PHILOSOPHY
AND
THE COMMON LIFE

BY

PAUL L. HOLMER

Professor of Philosophy
in the
University of Minnesota

THE TWELFTH ANNUAL KNOLES LECTURES

WIPF & STOCK · Eugene, Oregon

TULLY CLEON KNOLES

Wipf and Stock Publishers
199 W 8th Ave, Suite 3
Eugene, OR 97401

Philosophy and the Common Life
By Holmer, Paul L.
ISBN 13: 978-1-55635-793-0
Publication date 1/9/2008
Previously published by College of the Pacific, 1960

TULLY CLEON KNOLES
1876 - 1959

The Tully Cleon Knoles Lectures were established in 1949, three years after Dr. Knoles retired from the presidency of the College of the Pacific. During his retired life he found in the Lectures an occasion for intellectual stimulation. Baccalaureate and chapel talks reflected his reactions to the Lectures. The Lectures were a fitting tribute during his life and now are an appropriate memorial; for not only do they serve as a formal reminder of Dr. Knoles at each annual commencement, but, like the man in whose honor they are named, they also serve to stimulate us intellectually.

ROBERT E. BURNS
President
College of the Pacific

April 17, 1960.

CONTENTS

MODERN LEARNING AND MORAL RESPONSIBILITY

IT HAS BEEN often argued that learned men also ought properly to be the moral leaders of the race. Lest this conviction be interpreted simply as a statement of moral sentiment, let me hasten to add that most people who say this kind of thing are not simply being generous in moral wish; instead they are expressing a conviction dear to the learned, namely, that learning itself qualifies men uniquely for moral responsibility. If one has never heard this said on his own behalf, he has missed what is certainly one of the most histrionic and exciting sides of education. For few things seem so eloquent and moving, so fitting the treasuring of truth, as the clarion call to higher responsibility and new realms of ethical glory. And especially if these are said to be a function of education.

Learning and Morality

Two kinds of rude rejoinders come to such an attitude today. Both of them are from the learned world. On the one side, practitioneers in the respective domains of learning are increasingly aware that no ethical suasions, and certainly no religious dispositions, are a direct product of scholarship in their domains. With dispassionate calm, many of the scholars and scientists like to say that as important as questions of ethics and conduct are, they do not belong to their own province. These issues are then summarily dispatched to the philosophers. However, the philosophers deliver the second blow. Anyone who has that hungry look created by desire for a way of life is doomed to further disappointment. Even the ethicist among the philosophic tribe will say that they have nothing to assuage the fainting seeker; for philosophy is now understood not to proffer any pearl of great price, no wisdom, nothing by which to guide a man's behavior or even to suggest the next step. Philosophy is "about" ethical decisions and ethical talk; and rare, indeed, are the professional philosophers who are prepared to issue any commandments or disclose any loftier purposes for the perspiring masses.

All of this is sometimes written off as the shirking of responsibility and the denigration of the learned profession. Though one would be a fool to defend the entire crop of learned, still this kind of charge is wide of the mark. There is justification for the learned man's posture on these questions, and this justification also needs its hearing and occasional defense. For not every professor is an ethical fool, nor is every philosopher simply without courage and unequal to his high calling if he refuses to act as pontiff to the race. On the contrary, there are men of nobility and ethical poise, who speak with understanding and compassion, who say these things, negative as they sometimes appear, because of fidelity to learning and truth.

Furthermore, this pattern of learned abnegation is not fortuitous or casual. It is now confirmed by considerations drawn from a wide variety of fields and interests. The irony is that it comes not from the fideists, whom one could imagine enjoying the predicament that the confidence in knowledge has produced, but from all kinds of detached and circumspect students of the traditional areas of learning. So, the disparity between knowledge of what is and the convictions about what one ought to do is no longer described simply by philosophic dogmas; nor is it believed because of logical and systematic considerations, open only to a minority of the professionals.

Instead, it is almost a grass-roots matter—if one may be pardoned the expression. Today the view about the disparity seems to have more substance because it has grown out of wide learning and the meditations of large numbers of people. When John Dewey and other liberal thinkers of the recent past made a case against the two-story picture of reality, that of facts and values, they were meeting only one particular form of the disjunction. Dewey particularly seemed to relish the demolition of any view which so defined values that they were no longer in the context of nature and history. The refutation of the view which hypostasized values and placed them in ideal realms seemed to him to imply that values were tangible and accessible by the same means that facts were. Much of the enthusiasm which Dewey's naturalism created was not enthusiasm for that somewhat crabbed and circumscribed world view at all. Instead, Dewey gave a clue to all kinds of people about the mystery of ethical decision, and, furthermore, he articulated a very plausible program for which the available instruments of education seemed eminently suited. Unfortunately, however, Dewey's refutations were directed only to the metaphysics attributed to the fact/value distinction. Irrespective of the metaphysics, the distinction is still present and seems to demarcate one of the permanent diagnostic facts about the human condition. For the fact is that there is an unbridgeable logical gap between an "is" and an "ought." There are no scientific grounds for moving from one to the other, nor are there any cognitive grounds for deciding between two contradictory ethical positions.

The investment which some men of learning have had in scholarship and science is certainly a poor one. For often men have conjectured hopefully that a lack of morality or what they deemed bad morality would certainly be replaced in the course of learning. Everyone who talks Dewey's view of progress through more education is probably caught in this genial illusion. Now, however, it is quite clear that little really can be done in these matters. For the description of moral concern does not create it, nor does the truth about morality induce a sense of moral obligation.

This awareness has its painful side. For in the day when the solidarity of mankind seems a moral necessity and when the hankering for unanimity on a few matters of a moral sort seems to be a downright need, it is disconcerting to discover that moral resources are not stored up for use like the treasures of science and scholarship. We seem to be as unprepared for the large moral responsibilities involving nations and even the world, and as unprepared to resolve pervading moral differences, as we were in centuries of ignorance.

Just why this is so I would like to indicate in a few theses.

The Moral Neutrality of Nature and Culture

First, it is most clear that any attempt to ground the persuasion of men in nature is a major vanity. The odd fact of the matter is that the underived given environment, which we call nature, is seemingly equally compatible with any and all derived and artificial environments, which we call cultures. If nature allows all cultural poses, this is as much as to say that nature sanctions none of them. The grandly anthropomorphic views of the past which conceived nature as the warranting agent for law, for certain rights and privileges, and even for beneficences, is not corroborated by any kind of scientific evidence whatsoever.

Nature hides no plans for the future and suggests nothing of immediate use to a moral agent. If every privilege can be grounded in nature, this is the same, logically, as saying that no privilege can be grounded in nature. All the language which says that nature is a reservoir or a resource for moral inquiry, and every view which suggests that a law of nature is persuasive or even a sanction of positive law—these are certainly metaphysical at best; and such contentions no longer stand in any necessary relations to matters of fact. This is not to say that such views are meaningless; on the contrary, they are undoubtedly meaningful, but their meaning is no longer a function of science and scholarship and, certainly, is not a consequent of disinterested knowing.

The hope of the classic kinds of naturalisms now seems dissipated. Modern science, with its detailed accounts of the small parts of our cosmos, has not confirmed the naturalistic temper in its ways at all. For naturalism as a world-view has always expressed a

suasion too. Its persuasive view and perhaps motivational source
seems to me to have been the hope that a single and natural frame
of reference could be appealed to amid all the differences between
cultures and moral opinion. But now it is apparent that just as
nature itself (the stars, moon, rivers, animals, and sundry things)
is compatible with differing cultural and moral postures, so too is
the knowledge of nature equally compatible with these differing
postures. No longer can one appeal to the knowledge of nature
as the ultimate court of arbitration.

Nature itself seems neither to be moral nor immoral. The
distressing thing is that moral conviction and behavior belong to
people and not to other things. Thus a kind of bifurcation between
the natural order and moral behavior is fairly well established, as
well established, at least, as the difference between a thesis which
tells us the way things do behave and a thesis which tells us that
this is the way we ought to behave. Our praise and blame still
belong to people, not to stars and atoms, nor to molecules and cells.
And there is no ground available to us within the knowledge of
what is, for vindicating, in any definitive and indubitable way, our
praise and blame of people. Any vindication in virtue of principle
is always in virtue of moral principles; and these, in turn, are never
justified by anything non-moral, natural, or historical.

All of this is said while admitting that the social sciences are
very rapidly showing us that the fabric of human life is shot
through with moral judgment. While there have been grandiose
claims made about the social sciences, especially about the possibility of social engineering and of the control of human destinies,
still very solid contributions have also been made. We know now

something about the ubiquitous character of morality in every culture. Gone is the view, too, which claimed morality only for one culture. Every culture, in turn, has some kind of morality system, and social scientists are doing an admirable bit of work in describing the dimensions of the suzerainty of morality, also its effects, its causes and the deviations therefrom.

But all of this knowledge has not made moral judging any easier. Even if one admits that moral absolutes are untenable, still this view by itself does not mitigate the measurable differences between moral relativities nor provide a resolution of them either. Surely it is not true that we mean by a wrong only what our culture system suggests. The point is that those people who argue that morality is only an expression of a cultural system, and that anything inconsistent with the cultural system is wrong, are also mistaken in taking consolation in their cultural relativism. For, just as it is a mistake to use nature to vindicate a moral judgment, so too it is a mistake to use a culture to vindicate a moral view.

Furthermore, some cultures are also pluralistic on the moral side. They seem to permit a certain kind of amplitude and variety. But the irony does not lie here as much as it does in the juxtaposition of men and cultures, on the one side, and moral judgments, on the other. For moral judgments, in some way, have to be chosen and accepted. Some of them have to be chosen from among alternatives which are mutually exclusive and, certainly, no culture warrants the choice.

The moment a choice between value systems is made apparent—and this is what the cultural relativists have done for us by their description—no resolution of that choice is to be found in more facts. The question of the sanction of moral principle is as ambiguous and as difficult a question to resolve in the cultural sciences as it is in the natural sciences. In neither case is nature or culture the reservoir and resource for moral decision. Seemingly, the larger the cultural matrix becomes, the more diffuse and pluralistic the moral suasions within; thus the attempts to secure international cultural unanimity hold as slight promise, morally, as did the endeavors to know the entire physical cosmos.

The Gap Between Disinterested Understanding and Moral Interest

But there is another side to all of this too. Any kind of knowing demands a disinterested temper on the part of the knower, and any kind of morality supposes an interested temper. There is no cognitive bridge between these two tempers.

Knowledge demands certain conditions of the knower. The most important of these is detachment and disinterestedness. A claim we find necessary to make about all knowledge is that truth is independent of wish and proclivity. We insist that truth is objective, i.e., that the truth quality of any sentence is independent of any subjective disposition of the thinker and any value system of a culture. In order to know objective truths, it is essential that the knower also be objective. The practice of scholarly independence includes even an independence of whatever value system a man otherwise espouses; and, more than this, it calls for an objectivity about one's subjectivity.

But the perfection of a person morally demands something quite different. The moral temper is one of interestedness. Every man who suffers from an aberrant form of subjectivity, such as that of Don Quixote, is surely to be pitied. But the person who is without all subjectivity, or the one who has made objectivity and detachment the sole governing temper of his life, is surely mad in another way. Moral perfection does not mean anything less than the acquisition of a pervading enthusiasm and interest, adequate to every vicissitude of daily life.

The Stoics in the ancient world tried to invest controlled "apathy," the *apathos* state, with moral worth. They argued in a way that appeals to all rationalists, namely, that the maximally disinterested grasp of all that is would also entail, necessarily, the good life. Surely they were wrong; Spinoza even tried to argue that a new kind of love and passion would ensue in such circumstances. It is to the everlasting credit of the Stoics and Spinoza that they did have such moral enthusiasm that they succeeded in smuggling it into their reflections; but in neither case was the moral theory adequate to the facts of moral life.

Modern philosophy is surely correct when it says that the disposition and subjectivity of the individual is the arena of moral life. Neither nature or culture, when viewed disinterestedly and cognitively, has moral qualities. In fact, moral values are not predicates nor attributes of anything natural or objective. Perhaps these matters should be spoken of more guardedly—we do not know in objective fashion that moral qualities inhere in anything else but people.

In our objective cognitive posture, the world and things in it, even other people, can be objectively and truly described. However, all the descriptions of moral behavior, of good or bad acts, and of suasions or the lack of them, cannot move one from the disinterested understanding and posture to an interested participation and posture. The breach between tempers is wide and remains so no matter how great the quantity of knowledge. This is another way of saying that there are no necessary connections between knowledge of the world and attitudes we might have towards it. There are, of course, plenty of connections; but the connections are fortuitous, casual and individuated, never necessary. Again, we must note that the salvatory character of the knowledge stance is not borne out by careful examination. Morality is a perfection of interest, but morality seems like an emergent in the life history of the individual; moral passion stands in no necessary relations to what a man knows about the world, other people, or even himself.

Of course, all of this is a big part of the human adventure. We are still without objective warrant for moral decisions. Apparently there is no discernible advantage to knowing all of human history as over against the short span allotted to oneself; nor is any marked moral preferentiality given to those who look at big stretches of the universe as over against those who know only their neighborhoods. The gap between disinterested understanding and moral interest is as large for one man as another. One thing is clear. By enlarging the first, the second becomes no easier.

The Inner Life of Every Man

This is to say, then, that the talk about the grounds of morality, about moral resources, and even the scholar's responsibility for social change are, by and large, nonsense. The nobility of morality lies in the fact that it rests equally with everyone. In one sense of the word, there are no moral teachers, for there are no objective grounds and sanctions for the process of morality. In another sense of the word "teacher," there are moral teachers; but those who "teach" morality teach in another sense altogether—they elucidate by precept and principle another possibility which invites human concern. This latter kind of teaching is not a searching out of the objective grounds by which a new truth can be formulated or an old one can be justified and verified; instead, it is a matter of discerning those lineaments of what ought to be that some people need in order to be justified as moral agents. But the justification cannot be vicarious, and, finally, it cannot be done intellectually.

This is to say, too, that morality cannot be left to anyone. It belongs to everyone equally, and it is too important to be relegated from one man to another. But this may sound like the death-knell of civilization, a veritable invitation to more moral anarchy!

In our day there seem to be two major arenas open to our moral concern. On one side, we are all tantalized by the failure of moral values to control and to govern international behavior. Everywhere we find motives moving us in the direction of hoping for an international community where common moral interests will keep us from annihilating each other. The desperate situation in which men find themselves, where, in obedience to their respective best interests, they deem it necessary to fight and to kill, is not only physically repugnant, but it is also morally reprehensible. All of us hope that the scholar's independence of a cultural and national scheme of interests and values might enable him to tell us which is which.

But, I confess that all of this seems like a terrible mistake. However, it is not true that scholarship is so bound by the culture that everything inconsistent with a culture's value axiom is wrong. Indeed, scholars can be disinterested and independent; but the deeply ironic state of affairs is that disinterestedness does not provide access to interestedness. Disinterestedness is not the temper in which we apprehend moral principles. Human interests are not hypotheses—they are neither true nor false in any objective sense. All of the yearning for evidence for a moral view is really misplaced. When a man says that it is good for him to do so and so, his language looks like ostensibly true or false language. But if he is pressed and he knows what he is saying, he comes quickly to the point of admitting that his sentence does not matter—his interest is the moral locus, not the sentence. The truth or falsity of his sentence, if this can be ascertained, is irrelevant to the quality of interest which makes him moral.

There is still another arena for moral concern. It is the small arena open to each of us as individuals. No one has succeeded in discerning the teleology for the whole physical cosmos or the whole of civilization. Even the religious man, who says God causes everything to work together for good to those who love Him, must still say that this teleology is not evident. Throughout the learned world there seems to be a hazy notion floating about to the effect that a little more research and a little more learning will make it all clear. But, if anything has become clear at all, it is that the attempt to find a warrant for moral purposing in some teleological factor in the world and civilization is simply mistaken. We must return to the small arena, again, and take heart. The moral ordering of men must come from within and not from without.

All attempts to discover another level of reality, an ideal order, a regulative pattern, or even a divine being, which would warrant objectively the decisions we find it incumbent to make as moral agents, have come to naught. The enthusiasm some people had for metaphysics now seems to be drying up. Surely metaphysics is the endeavor to relate the whole of "what is" in a manner consistent with one's interests. But, for centuries men have hoped that metaphysics could be a disinterested science of reality by which their moral decisions could be ultimately guided. Now we know differently. Metaphysical views of the world are really depictions of the nature of things relative to our interests. Metaphysical schemes are transpositions from the small cosmos, to which we have individual access and in which we purpose our interests, to the large cosmos around us. Once people thought the business went the other way around, but they were wrong. Metaphysics is not the proof of the ethics—it is an expression thereof. It is an interested appraisal of the large cosmos, not its disinterested final science.

This is the upshot of modern philosophy, of positivism and analytic philosophy, to the educated man of our day. Metaphysics is dead if we mean by metaphysics the disinterested science of reality. Some philosophers went too far and said that it was nonsensical. This does not follow. Metaphysics is an interested study of what is, and it makes a great deal of sense; however, its uses are admittedly limited.

With the concerted criticism of the doctrines of final causes in the universe and of teleological explanation, we are still left with the small arena, the inner life of every man. Here it is necessary to have interests and purposes; and nothing objective reduces the importance of an inner teleology any more than it substantiates it in advance. Whatever has been done to and with a social group, morally and politically, has no better warrant than it has in the life of each man. It is a mistake to assume that bigger agglomerations of people have bigger objectives and referents for their views than do single individuals.

The vindication of the democratic conception of government (not always its practice) rests finally on the correct moral theory to which it gives expression. But here there are no values to be invoked or objectivities to serve as warrant. Democracy supposes that the will and interest of the individuals must be consulted before a general social teleology can be enunciated. Modern learning has done nothing to dispel the importance of this view. The short way in human history is always deceptive. In the wish to have the victory for all, a single moral aim and teleological goal is proposed. But this always violates the moral disposition of the individuals involved. The long way, which dignifies men even though it may threaten their civilization, makes the small arena of each man's life all-important. It suggests that the moral victory which comes to each man in turn holds the promise for the whole world.

Though there are many decriers of modern learning, who believe that it has reduced us to whelps crying for the father in the moon, I refuse to concede to this interpretation. Instead it seems to me that the dimensions of our common humanity are becoming clearer than ever. We have good reason to glory in being human. While it may be true that there is no warrant for confidence in the objectivities of nature and history, there is still the fact that each of us can bring our moral selves to birth. Through such a simplicity as this, the world's moral work is done.

If one considers the question of moral resources, it turns out then that these lie close at hand. Every man is equally proximate. We must learn to content ourselves with the maximal differentiation and development of each personality. Via such a prosaic and ordinary road, morality enters the world.

MORALITY AND THE INNER LIFE

For a variety of reasons, learned men tend to disparage subjectivity and the inner life. Over a century ago, Hegel even dared to say that there was something called "the bad subjectivity" which had to be overcome and vanquished before maturity would come about. And we all know the bad reputation which "being subjective" has in comparison with "being objective." For subjectivity seems to denominate the mad chaos of desires, of feelings, of wishes, which succeed one another in random manner and lack all cohesion and logic. No wonder then that most of us believe so strongly in the objective temper; for it usually succeeds in time a vagrant and whimsical subjectivity and often has at least shape and style. Let us consider why subjectivity has its bad reputation.

The Disparagement of Subjectivity

Crudely assertive egoists are one source of the bad reputation of subjectivity. Such egoists identify their private aims with the common good and seem unable to modify their goals because they are unable to empathize and to identify themselves with others. They lack the common measure and are, therefore, unable to find any means of disciplining their own assertiveness. In like manner, Socrates and others in the ancient world, who stressed certain rational endeavors, castigated very severely a group who were called

Sophists. In the estimate of their enemies, at least, Sophists were dreadfully subjective. They did not seem to distinguish between "opining" and "knowing." Sophists did not seem to be able to recognize the difference between something or other being the truth and the matter of believing. The latter act, namely, the act of avowing and saying "I believe" is, of course, a psychological occurrence. There is a marked difference, too, between saying, "I believe, therefore it is true," and saying, "It is true, therefore I believe it." Early Greek critics of sophistry try to state the criteria and the grounds for judgments like "it is true" in order to show that there are objective truths. Objective truths are true independently, many philosophers would say, of the psychological act of believing. Once again human subjectivity is brought into ill-repute, or perhaps we should say that in virtue of the ill-repute of human believing, its contradictory and often nonsensical content, the students of things human are inclined again to praise a kind of detachment and disinterestedness in contrast to what seems to be the wantonness of subjectivity.

Another feature of reflection about these matters is the now widespread consensus that subjectivity and all that make it up, passions, desires, believing, likes and dislikes, are so random and so chaotic that nothing more can really be said. Scarcely anyone is willing to challenge that consensus. We tend to agree that the inner life of men is like Charles Kingsley's caterpillar, squishy and squashy, with no fundamental structure, no definitive limits. I suppose that this is why romanticism in literature is thought to be by some people so desperate a phase of literary history. Irving Babbitt made a kind of literary mark for himself and a new but

slightly scandalous reputation for Jean Jacques Rousseau by link-
ing the latter to the romantic movement, which in Babbitt's learned
estimate was base, undisciplined, anti-rational, and subjective. Not
only this, though, for romanticism was also said to be individual-
istic and, hence, idiosyncratic, expressive and lacking the common
and inter-human and trans-human marks. For individualism is
sometimes another word and way to denigrate our subjectivity. To
say that a man is an individualist may mean that his motivations,
his beliefs, his goals are private and not finally open to adjudication
and discussion. Once again this seems to say that subjectivity means
privacy, and privacy means that no standards, criteria, or judgments
are possible.

Thus arise the strong convictions among men to the effect
that this kind of subjectivity, which is native, must itself be cor-
rected. It is not true simply that men make mistakes when they are
subjective and hence are judged because of their mistakes, but it is
rather that we are inclined to believe that subjectivity itself is the
mistake, that it ought to be supplanted. The strong urges towards
rational behavior, the continual barrage of conversation in learned
circles about education, about looking at both sides before deciding,
about consulting evidence, about being critical, these and many
more gambits of talk are tokens of the repute that subjectivity has
among us. It is not true that everyone who believes without warrant
believes wrongly, but it is not easy for us to credit such believing
with merit. Likewise, not everyone who acts spontaneously and
out of whim necessarily misbehaves, even by the most stringent
rules; but, I take it, most of us are inclined to think that such action
is an accidental phenomenon and that the individual can only be

made more responsible by being made less spontaneous and more objective.

This draws our attention, also, to a couple of features of contemporary intellectual life. The philosophers seem to have given up human subjectivity almost completely as a subject for study. Despite the whimsical and absurd manners of thinking among men, where fallacies abound and where valid argument occurs principally in logic textbooks, and despite the fact that the justification for arguments is something men discover long after they have the conclusions, still philosophers write books about the nature of thought and look for rules and laws and identities in language that we think is objective. In fact, philosophers seem to believe that there can be a science about thinking. Logicians have looked for universals and claimed to find them in our rational endeavors. It is almost as if the epistemologists and the students of reflection have said that we can discover and identify some common elements in our respective ways of being reasonable. The philosophers tell us that there are laws of thought, that there are universals somehow embedded in everybody's thinking or their language, that here there is something *entre-nous* which is public, non-idiosyncratic, and the veritable *sine qua non* of our human nature.

But this kind of rationality is not our raw human nature. When Immanuel Kant talks about our humanity, he speaks as if there is something shared by all men, as if individuals can be fundamentally characterized in their likeness. For him as for the major tradition of philosophy, dignity belongs to rationality. This can be described in categories and this is a kind of "addition," an increment to which men succeed almost at the expense of their sub-rational and subjective natures. Inclinations are to Kant uncomfortably individual and subjective. Kant, like so many others, sees a long and continuous war between the passions and inclinations, on the one side, and reason, on the other.

Rationality and a measured moral life are even free, Kant thought, of inclination. He spoke about autonomy and seemed to think that this meant that an ideally rational man would be the kind whose behavior could be completely described in rational categories. It would mean a life never motivated or activated by inclinations. So free would this ideal man be that no subjectivity would intrude and nothing idiosyncratic would ever find expression.

It is precisely this kind of thinking that abnegates too Kant's attempts at an autobiography. Ernest Cassirer, a life-long student of Kant, finally concluded that Kant could never pen an autobiography because to do so would mean an admission of something private and personal, something subjective, motivating him. This is a very strange view when you stop to reflect upon it, for it means that Kant was not permitting himself to write or to say anything about himself. Apparently his theory about reflection and reasoning made him suspicious of anything that did not fall under a category or fit a place within a schematism, and therefore autobiographical remarks were illegitimate. Perhaps it is to remark, too, upon the fact that Kant hoped that any language about himself might simultaneously be the language about an universal man, the man in men, the rational self. Kant suggested that each of us was dual. There was the phenomenal self, which was subjective, and the noumenal and real self, rational and objective.

Correlative to this kind of a view is another. Most of us are inclined to say that matters of the inner life are really the concern of the psychologist. Hence, today the more widespread our dismay over the prospect of making people rational, the more inclined many of us are to studying people to find out about their motivations. Often though this is done in virtue of a counsel of despair. Because most people cannot become objective themselves we are inclined, apparently, to believe that someone has to become objective and rational about them. Psychologists, too, have often agreed to study irrational and subrational and even unconscious behavior, some of them even admitting that such behavior was subject to clinical study, not statistical accounting; and some of them have gone further, suggesting that such behavior among men was really inferior, not quite up to the level of conscious and deliberate deciding and acting.

So again this has meant almost a relegation of human subjectivity. When contemporaries say, "that isn't a logical matter, it's only psychological," they apparently intend to bemean the matter under discussion by suggesting that here the speaker is subjective. Hence there are only idiosyncratic causes in which the psychologists are properly interested. Freud's discussions about the "id," which is subrational and a kind of seething mass of unconscious drives and forces, apparently seem to many readers to be the last word on the subject of human inwardness. Freud suggests that there is no real science and logic of the "id," but there are techniques and a strategy for its discovery and its control. Again the net effect is to negate our inner life, our subjective selfhood, and perhaps, too, to make suspicious something so dear to most of us as our self-concern. We are afraid that concern about ourselves, self-consciousness, might be that kind of Narcissism which can only spell further personal disaster.

All the moralistic and psychological patter about forgetting oneself, going out and enjoying oneself, stopping this morbidity, is also summarized in the rhetorical advice which says, in effect, go out and think about other things, get a little objectivity, try to see yourself as others see you. The plea is away from subjectivity and inwardness and on to objectivity and better mental states. These expressions seem like permutations on the familiar conflict which comes through much of modern philosophy. Descartes, Pascal, Hobbes, Spinoza, diverse as they were, nonetheless agreed that reason and the passions can only mean perpetual torment and conflict for everyman. Because the passions are very difficult to eradicate anyway, it seems a slight improvement in the history of the race now to be able to hope that psychological study is going to provide the clues to a means of control.

But, all in all, there is still a long-standing rebuke registered against our subjective selves. It seems a little odd too that education is so uncertain on the side of the passions. We are not quite certain how to educate human passions though we are fairly certain how to educate the intellects of our fellows. However, this brings us to another and very difficut issue, namely, whether the passions can be otherwise described and whether subjectivity is substantial and constitutive at all.

On Answering the Ethical Problem

If one tries to discover the rationale for the liberal arts and the general education we proffer the novices, one soon notes that human subjectivity has once again asserted itself. It is not that the rationale is whimsical or fortuitous, but the liberal arts are both a concession to the past and a concession to the way men in fact are as subjects. In truth, the liberal arts also deal with the constants among men, the concerns with man's destiny and duty. Yet a certain indirection seems to be practised. For the liberal arts—literature, music, and awareness of the great and creative minorities and their works—certainly do not instruct us directly in what we shall do or be. Yet the motivations, I suspect, of most learners and perhaps of most of the teachers, is to come as close as they can to discussing the problems and turmoils created by passions which need direction and goal. Hardly anyone is prepared to say, though, that such teaching will bring anyone into a new quality of life and a new sense of obligation and personal earnestness. This is at once to say too much; for the liberal arts, even though they traffic rather freely upon human feelings and desires, do not promise very much more than the liberty of choice.

The liberal arts are like the stars again, which might incline but do not command. Here the liberal subjects differ markedly from the sciences, natural, unnatural, social, or otherwise. For the sciences do command us, and they demand our attention and belief, albeit without really saying very much if anything at all to the questions raised by our subjectivity and inwardness.

Here a certain lesson can be learned even from watching the

way philosophers do in fact behave. Most young persons who study philosophy probably are motivated by questions loosely having to do with their destinies and their duties. By and large, it seems to me ethical and religious questions are very early the center of most intelligent people's concerns. But philosophers very soon seem to spend an inordinate amount of time and effort upon logical and epistemological issues. This, in fact, is a charge frequently leveled against contemporary philosophers by many critics, that the interests have become trivial, that secondary and peripheral problems are uppermost within the profession.

There is, I suspect, a reason for this hiatus between motivation and outcome. It may well be that intellectual maturation accounts for some of it. For some issues, though by no means all, do become upon closer scrutiny something different than one initially believed. Maybe some issues about duties and destiny, purposes and "what ought I to live for?" are capable of refinement and separation into finer and better discriminated questions. However, it does not seem that all of them are.

The discrepancy between motivating concerns and professional competencies among philosophers rests in part upon the very peculiarities of human subjectivity, the locus of our concerns and passions. Philosophers like everyone else begin with problems of the self, broadly speaking with ethical and religious problems. That they should end by talking about the logic of discourse, even the logic of moral discourse, or more likely the logic of science, seems a little odd. However, here too there is the discovery that argument and disputations, speaking and writing, are properly directed towards issues amenable to intellectual analysis. If we seek agreement through conversation and teaching, it seems that we can reach that agreement only on the basis of reasons presented. When one glimpses the possibility of a kind of truth which can be reached step by step, using defined facts and clearly articulated and cleanly chiseled reasons, one is eager both to clarify such reasoning for oneself and also to present that reasoning to others.

Loving thinking for its own sake comes very easily. Start where we will, with the most encompassing of hopes and grandest of wishes, still one cannot deny how frustrating these hopes and wishes are to handle. On the other hand, the discovery and exhibition of whatever propositions constitute the frame and the foundation of human knowledge is a sheer joy. The interplay of ideas, the clashes of doctrine, even the unpretentious discourse of polite conversation, invites a closer inspection of what is being said, how it is being said, why it is being said. It's not a long step to concerning oneself exclusively with the rules and procedures attendant upon marshaling reasons and providing decisive demonstrations.

A conflict then arises. The attempt to philosophize more disinterestedly, about matters of logic and the nature of knowledge, tends to replace progressively the very interests that engendered the pursuit in the first place. Also, and not in virtue of accident, it gradually dawns upon many thinking people, not least some philosophers, that ethical issues are not to be met by ethical doctrines or propositions. For one soon learns that whatever doctrines are presented to the mind as ethical are in all probability something else. Ethical convictions are not really there to be learned in the same way as other beliefs, propositions and doctrines are. To apprehend propositions, that may be connected one to another and demonstrated, is any thinker's task and delight. To argue about them with other thinkers is not only a delightful pastime but another way to make them clear to oneself. Somehow though the omnipresent ethical concerns, with which so much philosophizing begins, cannot be solved by logical analysis. Such issues do not have answers that can be demonstrated or even communicated to others as the terminus of a long chain of abstract reasoning. For, in the last analysis, problems of duty and destiny, important as they are, are not theoretical, epistemological, or logical problems.

Again the sceptre of subjectivism arises. For to say these things seems to suggest that therefore ethics is a matter of taste or a matter of private disposition. If not objective, then subjective— this seems to be the easy conclusion. And if what was said in Chapter I about morality and values not being read off the face of nature or out of the mores and social conventions of societies is the case, we seem to have left no other possibility than that of saying that moral issues are completely idiosyncratic and fortuitous. Moreover, it is certainly not essential to insist that there is or must be a radical separation between thought and action or between feeling and thinking. Anyone who turns to moral problems need not suddenly decide to emote and to give up thinking altogether. Neither is it discerning to say that moral concern entails a discontinuance of reflection and objective truth in favor of arbitrary feelings and private asserting and opining. This kind of dichotomous reasoning about objectivity and subjectivity falsifies the ethical issues.

Rather it must be said that thinking here illumines the problems, but it does not solve them. A thinking person can here discover what it means to be a man. He discovers all kinds of issues that must be met somehow and yet for which he cannot find or state, outside of himself, a conclusive answer.

It is almost as if philosophers have here made a fundamental category mistake. They perhaps share this mistake, it must be added, with many others. To turn the ethical inquiry into a search for the definition of the good may be what many philosophers have done. But this is not to respond to the question with which one initially began. However transparent and clear the definition is, however satisfying it is to oneself and others, it still does not answer the quest for destiny and duty. One must not misunderstand however. To say this is not to suggest that the question and concern was the wrong one in the first place. Sometimes philosophers have said that, and thereby they have separated themselves and philosophy from the masses of men. It is not clear, for example, that the original concern and question can really be translated into another one. Usually philosophers who do this substitute another issue altogether. On the other hand, it is not a mistake on the part of philosophers to settle for arguing about the consistency and adequacy of the definitions of ethical terms, or to wonder whether there are ethical examples which are properly abstracted or covered by the general terms. These are, after all, the proper areas for dispute, clarification, analysis and all the other things that we can do by thinking, talking, and arguing.

The mistake is to assume that answers proposed in philosophical doctrines have provided or will provide an answer to the ethical problems that living proposes for us. Since these latter answers cannot be said to be the outcomes of thinking, they cannot be presented to other men either as proved conclusions or conclusions subsequently to be proved. Ethical concerns are resolved in another medium.   They are resolved through decisions and choices not available to the objective temper of the onlooker. The point is that these ethical problems demand of us certain kinds and qualities of pathos and passions. We must learn to qualify our passions. Insofar as we educate on these matters of ethics, we really do it by exhibiting to others the ethical passions that are the resolutions of our conflicts and indecisions.

For this reason the liberal arts so often take us back to the domains of human subjectivity and passion. Within them it becomes appropriate again to look at human lives and to measure ourselves against them. Nothing is so irrelevant to the study of a mathematical theorem as the life and passions of the mathematician who first thought it up. The point is a simple one, for if he said something that was true, that truth is a quality of the theorem itself. Somehow the truth quality becomes apparent when one retraces whatever are the evidences or reasons for the theorem. All of these considerations lead one increasingly away from the mathematician and his personality. So too is it with logical matters, epistemological problems, the problems of history, the hypotheses of science. In all these instances where learning is to be had, where teachers can communicate to the learners, the psychological orientation is decidely away from the source, from the autobiographical, from everything subjective. The direction is toward a resolution of the problem outside of the thinkers altogether.

But this is not the case with these more fundamental ethical (and one might add again, religious) matters. Perhaps the liberal arts rightfully then cause us to consider the biographies, to consider the selfhood, the feelings or anything else that is being expressed in a created form. By and large here the direction seems to be quite different. We are asked to consider all kinds of facets of human personality, all kinds of pathos and commitment, which are not identical with, and cannot be produced by, thinking. Perhaps it is not altogether unwise that the liberal arts also be called the humanities, for in an indirect way, they project magnificently the possibilities which seem implicit in the rest of us. They make us realize as little else can that our lives embody a certain style and that no one is immune from this process of styling.

My concern here is not, nonetheless, to state a case for the liberal arts as much as it is to use them as an illustration of the importance and recognition of the place of human subjectivity. Ethical merit, to return to the main theme, we were saying, belongs finally to the very being of a man. Ethical doctrines are a poor substitute for the more fundamental matter of having an ethical passion and abiding commitment. Therefore to contemplate ethical doctrines and to worry about the nature of logical discourse or to be persuaded of the truth of ethical doctrines in the abstract might well be a very ridiculous matter.

To philosophers dominated by objectivist traditions all of this has invariably seemed to mean ethical skepticism or subjectivism. But I am suggesting something else. I have not the slightest doubt that there is a right answer to the ethical problem, but the irony is that since this "answer" cannot be demonstrated and presented as a conclusion, it cannot be discerned by thinking alone. Here human subjectivity must itself be exercised, and one of the ways to exercise it is to see where intellectualizing the difficulties leads one. The fact that there is no answer may lead one out of the skepticism to ethical insight. In fact, Kierkegaard went so far as to suggest that a despair about finding intellectual answers might lead a person to despair about the right thing, namely himself. When he did this, such a man might well be prepared to fashion a new and firm enduring ethical conviction.

Out of such dramatic conflicts within subjective and personal experience ethical qualities are born. This is what was argued earlier in words concerning morality being an emergent in the life history of the individual. Every person here too must work out his salvation, and the process is not without its fear and trembling. But just because the experience of subjectivity is a matter of disclosing the nature of that subjectivity and in turn a matter of determining that subjectivity, this experience lies at the opposite pole from whatever is capricious or accidental in the self. Thus we might say that in subjectivity we are not wallowing in the irregular or the inconstant. A new kind of objectivity is achieved by the persistent exploration of subjectivity. Like Socrates who found the expression "Know thyself" to be the means to ethical rationality, so too the claim is made here that finding one's destiny and duty is a matter of finding oneself. To grasp the subjective is not to apprehend true propositions about oneself or to know oneself as an object measured on the bell-shaped curve. It is, instead, to be aware of dramatic conflicts and to resolve them by living with conviction and passion a rich subjective life.

Moral Spontaneity

For this cause then morality must be considered anew in conjunction with the inner life. It is not enough to say that ethical judgments and value claims stated in terms of goodness and badness are simply statements of emotion and are thus only indices to the emotional life of the person making the judgment. This is to grab the stick at the wrong end, to specify the statements as if they were the fundamentals of ethical living. In what follows another kind of point will be made, wherein it is hoped that a fuller appreciation for the inner cosmos and its features will be realized.

Moral reformers from time immemorial have necessarily begun their task by attacking the rules and customs, the habits and conventions, in which morals have been taught. The prophets of righteousness of Old Testament history demanded a newness of life and a new depth to concern and passion. They rebuked the externalizing and congealing of morality in commandments and laws. They remind us that morality is not, after all, a matter of obedience alone. Even though catalogues of prohibitions and systems of injunctions are incitements to action, morality is never identical with what the system and the catalogue declare. Morality must always seek expression in action, but the action, obedient and legal though it be, is not enough for the genuine moralist.

All of us can have something better. Morality can and must be a fundamental inner attitude of mind and heart. It must also be a dominating enthusiasm, a spontaneity and an originating source of our conduct. Existing which is a mere repetition of other persons or which is mere obedience to the traditional and the customary is a denial of that very specific morality. Sometimes those persons responsible for the guidance of others insist upon obedience to a set of norms as the sign of morality. This is surely the easiest way to manage human behavior and it promises the most in the shortest period of time. But it fails lamentably in getting what we are after, namely, responsible moral agents. Jeremiah wrote long ago about the need for getting the commandments, which were already written upon tablets of stone, transcribed upon human hearts. I take it that he, too, was asking that formal obedience be given up in favor of a morality that was original and spontaneous in men.

This, of course, is but to say that morality supposes another kind of subjectivity. It is not enough to make demands upon another and then be satisfied with compliance, when we are really concerned instead for a new kind of inwardness in the person. It is possible, furthermore, to admit that the outward expressions of morality, laws and commandments, can change and must change with variations in circumstance. All kinds of factors relative to the culture, to the period in history, of status, of persons involved, might well produce differences in precept and rule. The inner spirit of morality aims at another kind of unity and identity altogether. For a dominating enthusiasm and a constancy within a man suppose an identity of the self with itself over the variety of circumstances and the long stretches of time. Again the mistake is to ask for the identity in the externals or the obedience to the same externals.

Thus one can say that initially morality is manifested to persons as a kind of social pressure. But the mistake is to assume that

this is all that morality is. From the standpoint of human inwardness the social demands are but imperfect disclosures of morality,
the by-product and not the thing itself. The more gentle expectations of certain kinds of conduct which are imparted to individuals by the groups to which he may belong are another case in
point. No one need deny that a kind of learning takes place in
such circumstances or that learning to obey conventions does not
have a salutary personal effect. Again, though, the moral life is
not really joined until the individual's response to these appeals is
firmly grounded in a person's subjectivity. What is meant here is
simple enough. Morality cannot be identified with the compelled
response even if that response is flawlessly perfect. Morality has
also to be a wish, a desire, part and parcel of human subjectivity.
Despite Kant's words to the contrary, morality can only be found
where there is a passion and an inward *telos* for obedience. Another
way that this might be described is to say that this response must
be freely grounded, voluntarily elicited, before morality becomes
an inner spirit of human life.

The language of morals and the language about morals by
the philosophers sometimes omits this somewhat evanescent characteristic of moral life. Philosophers, like other talkers, endeavor
to keep the business of morality flexible and negotiable to talk
itself. But the truth about these things is that moral earnestness
and enthusiasm are not the same as the words about them. The
idea of the good is itself disinterested and detached from human
subjectivity, but goodness itself is a form of subjectivity, a kind of
pathos. The idea of the good is not good. Words may be about
subjectivity but are never a substitute for it. The questions which

men raise about their destiny and their futures are not really questions about the nature of the good or the qualities of obligation. For philosophers cannot argue or delineate the goods of the subject life. These must be achieved by another means altogether. Ethical theories might well try to specify these things, but ethical theories are not incremental to the goodness itself; for ethical theories do not imply a net increment to the subjectivity, only to the objective grasp of related matters.

Moral codes are usually only average outward expressions of the inner spirit of the moral life. Codes are never exhaustive of the significance of a lively morality nor are they ever valid *per se.* Anyone who loves another in marriage knows a large number of rules governing that relation. Some of these are quite explicit and plain in command. But there are also a large number of expectations that come one's way through one's complicity in social life. For example, one is expected to remember St. Valentine's Day and the birthday and the wedding anniversary. And these may not be all. However, a man would be a moral fool if he thought that these rules and expectations were exhaustive of the moral side of marriage. For there are literally an infinite number of ways of fulfilling one's moral relation. The person who merely obeys the expectations does not begin to exhaust or to test a genuine enthusiasm called love. With a redoubtable tenacity, a moral kind of love keeps rising to every occasion and does not demand a plan in advance or a blue-print for the morrows.

No one can deny, on the other hand, the value of the conventions in themselves. Lessing long ago noted how conventions and habit also are the moral teachers of the race. But the reduction of morality to a set of habits is also the death of morality. Habits are often nothing but past moral experience, typified and now separated from the inner life. So, taught as we are by convention initially, the moral spirit in us always means a substitution of inwardness for externality. A routinized moral life is really, therefore, a contradiction in terms.

Externals and the Choosing Self

Another matter also presses for our attention. There is abroad in the land the view that happiness is a matter of fortune, of chance, of destiny. As a boy I remember seeing a book in the family library with the title "When My Ship Comes In." The hard cover of that book had a 'Turner-esque' picture on it of a ship looming up in the fog as it was approaching the harbor. When I asked my mother about that picture, she told me that the harbor was the harbor of life. A while later I read the book and found it to be a little bit sad, for it turned out that the ship never came in at all. In a kind of crude way, that title tells a story about a great number of people who are so living that they are everlastingly waiting for something to happen to them so that they, too, can become happy.

The Epicureans talked about fortune, the Stoics about destiny, others have awaited the visitations of God; and in ancient times and contemporary, happiness is believed by large numbers of people to be dependent upon what happens to a man. Thus men bless or curse their inheritance, physical and social. They enjoy or denounce their talents, their circumstances, their state of health, for it is upon these relativities that most of what passes for happiness seems to depend.

Morality makes a difference here that is all encompassing. Instead of measuring happiness in terms of what happens to a person, a moral enthusiasm measures happiness in virtue of what comes from a man. Instead of happiness being a function of what seems almost like a choice made for us, whether spoken of as Lady Luck's smiling upon us, Dame Fortune's choosing of us, or our hereditary and given advantages, moral enthusiasm seeks to live by the power of choosing. The discrimination that matters is the one of the man, not whatever discriminations were made in advance for him.

In this sense, then, moral men begin to live in the conviction that the issues of life, its good or ill, depend ultimately on the manner in which we use our powers of choice. Increasingly the way swings off, away from threading one's way through the obstacle course, hoping for as much happiness as events and one's own nature will permit, to another view, that whatever the circumstances and the limits of the self, that happiness comes within and by the act of choosing.

For then the goods of life are not the things around us nor is goodness a measure of the quantity of anything given us and evil a measure of that which is absented. The point is again that human subjectivity is once more made the locus of good, depending as it does then upon the energy of human pathos and not on something outside of the self. In this respect it must be noted that choice does not mean here a choice between things or even a choice between good and evil. For in the ethical way of life, good and evil are not externals—they are not qualities to be discerned in nature or history. So, good and evil are not anterior to the choice but are determined by the choice.

This is why a moral consciousness is not only an inner enthusiasm but is also that which discriminates and evaluates life in terms of choice. It is not enough to describe morality as an enthusiasm or as a passion and leave it there. This strengthens the frequent charge that morality is only a feeling and that moral laws are only feelings made public. The function of moral enthusiasm is invariably in the direction of evaluation, but it is certainly the subject who must evaluate. This is why a moral man does not accept existence as if its conditions were already completely chosen, for the sign of maturity is also to posit good and evil in virtue of an act of choice. These do not exist unless posited, and many of the ethical mistakes men make can be traced to their failure to recognize this. The highest stretch of human ideality is to be found in this single capacity of choice. Whatever worth and dignity we have as persons is concentrated right here.

Oftentimes we admire men for their genius, for their power and even for their fame. But if human worth is measured ethically and if it is measured by a deeply moral consciousness, then the essentially human factor which is the greatest potential, the most crucial area for discernment, is the area of choice. To have chosen to be an ethical subject, to have chosen to be a self, to have chosen to be a subject qualified and stimulated by one's own choice, this is the highest accomplishment for ourselves and the highest thing we can say about one another.

For the choice of being a good man, of converting a possibility into an actuality, is far superior ethically to converting actualities into possibilities. To return for the moment to the notion of sub-jectivity, it is almost as if men must choose for themselves that ideal self that they wish to be. The social pressures and expectations may project one kind of ideality for one, and the limitations of heredity and environment may seem to limit the range of possi-bilities considerably, yet it is still the self that must discover and define ultimately the selfhood that will govern all the rest. Thus the fundamental ethical choice is the choice of the self. An ethically defined subjectivity protests any limitations that can be objectively discerned and seeks to make all the objectively given raw material of human life, everything the psychologist and physiologist might measure as our individuality or individual differences, the very matter which must be conformed to the demands of the ideal self.

This in fact is what the process of moral life becomes—a transformation of the raw material into the ideal self chosen by that self. The distinction between good and evil is surely but a means to discriminate further that process and bring the self to birth. What men call values are not objective things anterior to man's appearance. Contrariwise, values are given by the evaluator and come to permeate everything man touches and makes because they are created by his discriminating the idealities for his own selfhood. By this means, enriched by an indwelling enthusiasm and moral consciousness, the ethical self is a concrete historically con-ditioned self, not an empty or mystical abstraction.

Neither is it correct to say that the moral man is simply self-created. For a moral consciousness, again, seems to me to be char-acterized by the thought that all of this is like a voyage of discovery. The ideal self is not an idle invention, a whimsical creation of an overstimulated and hot intelligence. Nothing romantic or episodic is here proposed. Again Kant is a good reminder of moral sobriety in this issue. Is it not the case that deeper penetration into human subjectivity really shows one that there are also universals in subjectivity? Are all of the universals epistemological and logical? I take it that a moral consciousness proposes another and long preoccupation with subjectivity itself to see if there is not something fundamental and inter-subjective within subjectivity too.

For our admonitions and entreaties, our appeals to one another, also have a kind of relevance. Some thinkers have too quickly concluded that these features of social life are a consequent of our ignorances and our failure to develop the properly objective techniques. But I should suggest that the painful and admittedly tentative ethical manifestations in human behavior ought themselves to be studied. Instead of ethical theorists only searching out the features of ethical judgments and the peculiarities of ethical rules, which of course will show features amenable to logical and disputatious interest, it might also be appropriate, occasionally at least, to have the universalities in pathos, in passion, and enthusiasm marked out. The point is a slight one however. For instead of investing ethical philosophizing with maximal importance because it isolates universals and antecedent-consequent relations in our ethical discourse, it would be more salutary to have that kind of analysis also show us that the discourse and its analysis is important when considered against the fact that ethicality really demands that our passional life be universalized, that our inner 'postures' and feelings be tuned to a non-idiosyncratic morphology.

The universals that are present in our discourse can undoubtedly be argued about and ought to be with resoluteness and clarity. But a man of ethical suasion seeks something more than this. He wants also a kind of personal and intimate worth and validity. He wants to be a good man, and a good man is not an intellectual achievement, perpetrated in discourse or by argument. This kind of goodness must be earned through discipline and struggle. But it is the idiosyncratic subjectivity, the impulses and odd incitements which must be controlled and fashioned into character. The critics of subjectivity are right when they distrust the undisciplined and vagrant areas that William James called the "blooming, buzzing confusion." This is precisely what they are. Ethical maturation is, however, not letting externals and objectivities rule the human spirit, but rather bringing to birth in oneself, within subjectivity itself, a new self, a positing and choosing self, whose determinations are the guides to living.

Subjectivity cannot be repudiated. It must be subjected to discipline and to transformation. However much the social pressures and laws help to bring about a suppression of the "bad subjectivity" of which Hegel and others have spoken, this is only a part of the task. For a new center of excitation, not only obedience, is the aim. That persons can have this as ethical men, in the presence of regulations and commandments, is testimony to the depths of subjectivity and the mystery of being a man.

MORALITY AND SOME INTELLECTUAL
CONSIDERATIONS

LONG SINCE, STUDENTS of human behavior
have noted that duties are clearly plural in number. All of us
acknowledge a long list of duties, frequently more than we can
satisfactorily undertake. Too, we usually accuse others of being
negligent of specific and several duties. We do not usually say that
a man has neglected his duty in general, though when it is sometimes said, it is said by way of summary and with rather clear intent.
We usually say that a man has neglected this or that specific duty.

The Source of 'Ought'

Such ordinary usage continues to be appropriate because
duties occur empirically in the plural. We know many which
originate in connection with very special circumstances. For
example, when an accident occurs, duties in great numbers arise.
We must note what occurred and how, we must help someone,
report accurately, etc. Sometimes duties as they occur to us are
difficult to understand in relation to other duties; for the very
circumstances which seem to bind us to help a wounded person on
a highway are the occasion for the law declaring that our duty is
otherwise, that we should let matters and bodies rest until a doctor
arrives. Still duties flow in upon us in a variety of ways, and there

45

is a peculiar kind of vulnerability to these that characterizes some members of the human family. One of the ways to control the occurrence of plural duties is to keep the circumstances predictable; and whatever the latter tactics are worth morally, they certainly are helpful in reducing the total number of duties which we must acknowledge.

Furthermore, we create duties by the promises we make. The promise to lecture at a given date and time is an incumbent duty. A relation between promises and duties is not simply a terminological matter, though the very words are, of course, extremely important. It is a moral phenomenon, important to be alerted to, that our promises do increase our duties, and the more the promises, the more the duties.

Our relation to other persons and all of the institutional forms that these take are also productive of distinctive requisites. Status as parent creates duties towards the child and vice-versa; rulers are duty oriented towards the subjects; teachers are, in virtue of their role, respectfully committed towards the students, and one would like to believe that something reciprocal obtains. Expressions of respect, of deference, of payment, are correctly adumbrated in the language by the prepositions. We incur obligations 'by,' 'to,' 'for,' 'with,' 'from.' Out of reflection about these facts, everywhere present, philosophic persons have isolated the characteristic of 'oughtness,' of obligation. We say, therefore, that men 'are obliged,' 'have obligations,' or that they 'ought to do such and such.'

A question has often been raised about plural duties, namely, whether there is not such a thing as a duty in the singular? But the relations have never been altogether clear. Is there a fundamental

obligation from which the plural obligations derive their oughtness? Some persons have said, albeit carelessly, that the plural
duties have come about in time, that they are imposed in the manner suggested, and that that is all that should be said. The only
question, then, is whether the human flesh is willing to respond and
if so, how it will respond. The locus of obligation lies obviously
outside of the man, so the report goes, and morality is a matter of
responding.

Other theorists, perhaps even more positivistic in philosophic
and legal bearing, have insisted that obligations root ultimately
in some human subjects, in their desires, and wishes, and that they
get subsequently translated into laws, institutions, and the more or
less solemn pacts governing societies and men. These external
expressions are really the human wishes a few times removed and
properly acculturated.

At the other extreme, there have been thinkers, who in their
anxiety to show that obligation is not so coarsely subjective in
origin, have insisted that there is a natural law, prior to wishes and
legislation, from which an obligation *per se* derives. This view
grounds obligation in a kind of trans-empirical and trans-subjective
law, a metaphysical demand, to which empirical human beings
are intractably related. Kant, again, argued that there was a single
imperative which was categorical and invariant which could be
discovered, not made, by reflection upon the plurality of obligations. By reasoning, he argued, one discovers the logical-like and
absolutely pure, that is to say, non-subjective and non-empirical,
character and origin of the categorical obligation.

However, it seems to me that such objectivist views are mistaken. The plural obligations indeed are derivative, and philosopher moralists are right to seek out their derivation in a single obligation. But it is clearly a mistake to look for that derivation by looking outside of the human subject. In order to avoid the absurdity of identifying each obligation simply by ascribing each to a whim and fancy, the ethical theorists have sought the objectivity of obligation in something outside of the human subject. The irony is that ethical objectivity, for there is such, is to be found in subjectivity itself. In this instance, we can say that there is a fundamental obligation-consciousness in the moral subject. This belongs to him, not in virtue of circumstance, status, or an accidental differentiation, but in virtue of his being a man. The plural obligations or duties derive their oughtness from this fundamental and qualified consciousness.

Such a kind of consciousness is part and parcel with the process of learning to evaluate by making choices. Such consciousness presupposes an inner enthusiasm which is moral and not simply *la joie de vivre* or a native exuberance. Therefore, this kind of consciousness is learned and is a matter of maturation. But neither chronological aging nor learning about this and that detail are sufficient conditions for a well-developed moral consciousness. The latter depends upon self-discovery. And this brings us back again to the issue of obligation.

For men are heirs to a very deep-seated need for a justifiable way of life. However, the scrutiny we can give ourselves can also be avoided. All of us want to be liked, and the world has long since learned how to make this superficial need mutually profitable. But a more fundamental twist is given to this matter when we turn upon ourselves and ask whether we ought not to be altogether different. This, too, can be put off, and some moralists, like Pascal, have believed that the inveterate thirst for amusements and recreation reflects the fear of a self-revelation which might occur if we are not quickly and thoroughly diverted. Certainly no significant moral stature is expected of children because they do not yet have the gravity of mind by which to assess themselves. Many people remain like children because their living is a series of diversionary moves by which they refuse to face their need for personal righteousness.

For righteousness is what men need. Men cannot bear a life which is not justifiable without a sense of guilt. Men have a need for a defensible happiness, and they need a kind of valid and universal selfhood. All of this seems to me what is meant by the need for righteousness. The sense of obligation is, in part, born of this need; for we are obligated to be righteous and to do the right. 'Ought' is rooted within that need of every subject self to have a justifiable way of life. The process of learning is, as we all know, many-sided, but nothing within the process is so important as becoming moral. We simply do not know how to make men moral, though we do know something about how to make them obedient. My suspicion is that the reason we do not know is that there is really nothing to learn. For every man must somehow come to these things by himself. The self is like Aladdin's lamp which must be traversed and rubbed by the person himself. When the need for righteousness occurs as a personal requirement, when it does not need righteousness for anything save its intrinsic worth, then the sense of obligation begins to grow too.

The 'ought' declares too the rightness. So we say frequently that a person ought to do something, for such an action is right. This has caused moralists to wonder whether rightness by itself is not a quality to be perceived and, hence, whether obligation is not derivative psychologically from the autonomous awareness of rightness. But this is to be misled by the language. Rightness springs from the subject's need and describes the kind of satisfaction which a moral consciousness can envision as justifiable and defensible. This is not to say that this envisioning is an intuition of an objective rightness, for that is another issue altogether. Neither is it to say that such rightness is merely subjective, again in the invidious sense. It is to say that rightness is here a discovery of a moral consciousness which is as objective and trustworthy as the intellectual and logical consciousness of men. From such a consciousness and enthusiasm, for both terms are appropriate, the obligations spring forth.

Obligation and the Inner Life

Another feature of obligation must also be remarked upon. For we also speak of a moral life as one acknowledging a debt, as one in which we repay what we owe. Again there are the pedestrian facts of owing for this and that, in virtue of contracts, promises and like. These are, however, only the point of departure, not the point of arrival, for a moral consciousness.

A profoundly moved man is profoundly moved because the stimulus is not a visible one. I suppose we speak this way because we are surprised to discover people whose motivation can not be easily discovered. Either we think them to be chaotic individuals who literally do not know what motivated them because they are not clear about themselves; or we think people with hidden motives to be really profound and mean by this that their motivation is somewhere deep in themselves.

Certainly there are people included in this group who do not think their obligations are fulfilled by doing their respective tasks. Once the jobs are done something else seems to create a demand. Of course, there might be people who are mentally sick like that too, but this observation does not begin to touch the crucial issue. For it seems possible and indeed plausible for a moral man to consider his whole existence as a task to be fulfilled. A sense of obligation then includes as one of its aspects the viewing of oneself as not completely independent or self-positing but as also owing. One therefore needs to repay a debt, and a life-time is often too short to discharge this kind of debt.

There is a kind of theory of ought as debt which says that this sense of duty is an expression of the relation between a higher and lower self or of the relation between reason and passion. Certain kinds of social absolutists tend to ground this sense of duty as debt in the fact that individuals owe society, i.e., that individuals are dependent upon the social group, and that the demands of a society create the sense of obligation. Moral nihilists and skeptics tend to argue that the ought as debt will dissipate as time goes by. The theses here are numerous and include the view that ought is a survival from days of the autocratic organization of society and the view that debt is a psychological artifact created by societies in the interests of securing allegiance and conformity.

Whatever the truth and falsity of views about origins, it seems to me that the most important matter is to discover the sense of duty as debt as rooted freely though firmly within consciousness. Whatever the route by which it gets there, and there are undoubtedly many routes, the issue is, What is to be done about it? Again a moral man tends to avow the debt and use this avowal to fulfill and to define his personal destiny. Obligation is surely an emergent in the life history of a person. A moral man grasps this debt-consciousness and makes it motivating. This is why his motivation remains hidden and why he is thought to be profound. Here, however, there is nothing intellectually complex that makes him profound; instead it is simply the hiddenness of his sense of debt. He owes without incurring a debt, this because he dares to view himself as a gift, not a self-derivation, and hence there is an always appropriate task.

Moral obligation is not then an imposition or a compulsion. It does not thwart or distort a man, nor need it be conceived as a limit upon a man's freedom. On the contrary, such an obligation, which intends to envelop all the other obligations and tasks, is the law of man's inner being and both defines the ideal self towards which he moves and directs the actual self which he is. Here obligation and freedom are not antithetical. Perhaps Aristotle's remark about perfect freedom being perfect obedience to perfect law is appropriate to these considerations. If one tries to understand his saying by reference to a natural and metaphysical law, or to a positive and legislative law, or to the will of the community, he seems to me to speak nonsense; but if the law is the obligation as above described, there is no difficulty whatsoever.

It is not amiss to note what practical moralists through the ages have said about this matter either. For Cicero, Pascal, La Rouchefoucald, even Francis Bacon, have noted all kinds of salutary psychological values which follow from a wholehearted recognition and espousal of obligation. Instead of stultification and desperation ensuing, the individual finds that a pervasive sense of obligation strengthens the will and orders diverse impulses into some kind of pattern. The impossible becomes possible.

Also, there is a kind of fittingness to being free of opportunism and not having to trim one's sail to fit every wind which blows. The very calculus by which men otherwise have to guide their life is gone at an instance when the sense of obligation takes over. Hence consistency, unity, and a single-mindedness ensue and give psychological equanimity. Perhaps it is not irrelevant to note that this is undoubtedly what most people seek as 'a purpose for life.' However crude the expression, it still bespeaks the dismay that so many feel when there is plenty of behavior, perhaps almost too much stimulation and too much responding, but what is lacking is some kind of principled control and delimitation. All this a sense of obligation provides. It is well to remember that one cannot prove an obligation to be obligatory, but one can confirm it in an appropriate way. To discover that it brings personal validity, a new selfhood, and a set of tasks is its confirmation. Anything less must be rejected. Because it gives hope, since there is always something to do, the sense of obligation remains pertinent to every vicissitude.

The Inner Source of Moral Principles

We must admit with the sages of yesteryears that the occasion for the sense of obligation and the need for a principled way of life is to be found in the raw stuff we call human nature. To this extent we must take the decriers of subjectivity seriously. For there is a kind of anarchy created by momentary impulses and passions. Without a guiding idea and a ruling principle every person who understands himself at all feels the lack of inner continuity. But the question is whether that guiding idea and rule is not also intrinsic to personality, as intrinsic as we ordinarily describe impulses and passions to be. The argument here has been that the sense of obligation is also rooted in the life of subjectivity and that its ordering is not an inhibition from the outside.

The evils to which we allude when we talk about desires and passions are not always the consequences of desire and passion. In fact, the presence of desires and passions does not promise an obviously evil social train. Bertrand Russell has humorously remarked upon the harm that good men do and noted too the good which evil men do. He is here remarking upon the fact that there is an incommensurateness between motive and accomplishment, such that one cannot safely infer from consequences to the moral quality of the doer or vice-versa.

The evils of passion and desire lie rather in their tendency to dominate the individual completely. This is, surely, an anthropomorphic way of speaking, but it says a great deal nonetheless. The passions seem like powers that sweep over us and usurp the abilities of discrimination and judgment. They are of the moment but their authority seems absolute. This, as I understand the matter, is the fundamental protest. Consequently the passionate and desiring person is heedless of actual social and physical connections and consequences—this cannot be denied. Again though, the fault and damage is the effect upon the person, for there is almost a complete destruction of perspective and a terrible undermining of all responsibility.

Even our language reflects some of these considerations. We understand 'pleasure' to be a passional good, momentary, and anarchic. Pleasure usually describes a part, a good of a part, in isolation from everything else. Happiness, instead, describes that more inclusive and organic kind of satisfaction, where the connections and totalities are acknowledged. Perhaps we might say, too, that the whole person, his memory and his hopes, does not have to be forsaken to suffer moral happiness, whereas the requirement of momentary pleasures is often that we forsake the remembered past, the standards to which we are otherwise dedicated, even the hopes for our tomorrows.

In relation to such mundane questions as the quality of satisfactions, then, morality and the moral consciousness bring a great deal to bear. Morality means in large part trying to interpenetrate everything, pleasures and pains, all of the random happenings, with a spirit of universality. Several things are meant by this expression and we shall allude to each in turn.

A moral man must look for a guiding and ruling principle. The spirit of universality is exemplified in the fact that he repudiates momentary satisfactions in favor of a principle valid for all times. What ancient writers, particularly the Stoics, called 'resignation' is surely part of all morality, not only Stoicism. It means the resignation of one's particularity in favor of a universal. Further, the moral agent searches out that kind of inner continuity, that constant and yet flexible obligation (flexible because it fits all things) which will bind impulses into principle. Translating this pursuit into language is another kind of activity altogether, but when moral men speak, they speak in behalf of principles, not impulses. Again though, it is a mistake to assume that a principle must be abstract and objectively derived in order to achieve universality. Ethical principles are universals *in re* within the subjectivity of the moral man.

Something else that is meant by ethical universality can be noted in the gradation and hierarchy of values that are constructed. A well-conceived morality puts universal and generically human values above differential values and goods. The differences among persons, which differences admittedly do create values, are all considered to be mere relativities. Thus even the esthetic values, dear to the sensitive man, are deemed inferior to values like faithfulness, courage and others, which anyone can have together with the most esthetically undifferentiated and insensitive individual. The task is to interpenetrate his own peculiarities with universality and to read himself back into the human race. Perhaps everyone of us cherishes some secret and inner incommensurability by which we believe ourselves to be different, if not superior. Some person's incommensurabilities are large and domineering, but the same task applies to all if morality wins out, namely, to see these *differentia* as imperfections, relative goods and not the major good. Morality means the demand to search out the likenesses between oneself and another and to excel right here. Morality forces every man, with whatever talents and vocation, to realize a task not given by his talents or his vocation, but one given by moral obligation.

In this respect morality stresses the duty of every man revealing himself and making himself intelligible to everyone. This is why morality brings about rules and commandments. These help a moral man declare himself and identify his own springs of action. This is the way that we can turn our lives into a book that all may read. For nothing is quite so suspicious to a sensitive moral consciousness as an action which cannot be explained. Idiosyncratic behavior, which is rooted in differences among men, is precisely what moral men fear. This is the 'bad subjectivity' again. In protest, a moral man believes it to be a greater and a more noble thing, also a happier thing, to be a man than to be a genius or to be talented.

All the excusing which goes on behalf of ourselves and others when we say, "No one understood me," "he is different than the rest," "his is an artistic temperament and he ought to be excused," these and more can be cited as instances of that which morality abhors. The differences among us are indeed very great, but morality claims to isolate the universal and common task. And this task is incumbent and can be discovered only by penetrating below the differentiating subjectivity and discovering the obligation, the self, the rule and needs that are there.

Closely related to all of this is the stress in morality upon social continuity and community. Here again the universal motif seeks expression by making it a duty to forsake one's asocial isolation in favor of brotherhood. The stress is upon the supremacy of what men do have or can have in common, instead of stress upon the advantages and values, even the perfection of privilege. Thus, the moral suasions tend to bind men in a universal brotherhood. The theme of the Stoics, *'homo sum,'* 'we are men,' is a kind of ground swell expressing the ardor and zeal of men in contradistinction to the pride that goes with being Roman, Greek, Russian, or American.

Aristotle's discussions about the conditions necessary for happiness and the practise of virtues leave little doubt that to Aristotle, at least, only the privileged few could be truly good men. In the *Nicomachean Ethics,* especially Books III and IV, he shows that the kind of goodness he has described is dependent upon wealth, upon friendship, upon a strong body, upon subtle psychological qualities, many of them if not all beyond the call of the will. The upshot of his book, then, is a case for a kind of *eudaimonia* that cannot be had by all and that can never even be expected by the vast majority. Even the *eudaimonia* is aristocratic.

Against all of this there is little to be said if Aristotle's book is considered to be only a description of the way things really are. For surely most of mankind, from Aristotle's time to the present, guard their privileges, physical, economic, and otherwise, as the only guarantors of happiness. Only a person stirred deeply by the inequities that are suffered and willing to forego his own privileges in order to seek a common good can significantly protest Aristotle's account. The 'ought' of morality is in another direction, namely, to discover a more fundamental community in which all may be members and equal sharers, irrespective of contingent factors.

The Morality of Work

We have been considering a few of the aspects of morality which have continually teased men into reflection. Notions of obligation as rightness, of obligation as debt; of how obligation principles and controls judgments and motives; of how morality elicits concerns with universal values—these certainly are perennial intellectual interests aroused by the moral life. But here I want to turn reflection to a very concrete and specific matter. Intelligence can move from instances to generality, which we have been doing, but it also can move from general considerations back to the specifics.

The matter to which I shall refer is the difficult business of working for a living. Recently it was publicly remarked that social planning has now gone so far that most people seem to take for granted the wisdom of a policy which says that farmers on unproductive land must be moved to more productive land, where their labor will be of greater utility, their lives useful, their days not spent in vain. Whatever the merits of the planning, there are serious matters to be joined in discussion of the forms of livelihood. We seem to forget very often the omnipresent ethical factors, and a moral consciousness is precisely that kind of consciousness which finds them everywhere, even in ordinary matters like that noted.

Popular lore has it that working is a chore and a curse, as if it is one of the requirements to be overcome but never satisfied. The current social situation in Western countries has forced us to consider retirement programs and the peculiarities to be met in the cessation of work and consequent forced leisure. Little of this reflection seems to be directed to the moral side of the matter of work. Moral considerations and the public media continue to be profoundly incommensurate. Even when some speak of work as something preferable to leisure, they frequently talk about its therapeutic values, that it keeps one busy, that one lives longer when working, that it keeps one young.

Again I take it that a well-grounded morality conceives of working for a living as a real perfection in human life, not at all the dire necessity it is so frequently construed to be. For work is one of the ways to give substance to one's duty, to give specific shape to one's ambitions and goals. There is, consequently, an obligation to work, again the obligation being grounded within the personality. Therefore the privileged circumstances which do not require that one work are ethically humiliating, and one can only be redeemed from such circumstances by setting oneself more taxing responsibilities than those required of normal men. The practice of working so hard that one will work his way out of work is also a dubious aim, ethically speaking. For the privilege of a well-earned leisure is, ethically speaking, an opportunity to undertake more demanding responsibilities. Such dearly bought freedoms can only mean a deepened sense of obligation.

The greatest foes to the enobling side of work are not the uncertainties of the livelihood, poverty, and the question whether the job will still be there, but rather the tendencies within a man to let himself be degraded by slipping from his duty and his sense of calling. But to say this is already to touch the nerve of all kinds of problems. Persons in privileged positions, fortified by prestige, power, money, and perhaps religion, have invariably found it easy to talk about the virtue of work and the salutary effects of battling economic insecurities. On the other hand, the underprivileged have perhaps too quickly identified themselves with the pursuits of security and proximate goals, as if these were all there were to be had. What are so easily forgotten, either with the privileges or without them, are the satisfactions of the inner man. For the inner man, the moral man, can find an immense satisfaction in exercising the weapons of the spirit in the battle for a livelihood.

Political considerations not withstanding, it is always wise, again ethically, to think about these aspects. But the thinking perhaps ought to be on one's own behalf, not one's neighbors. It is a question whether one's work should not be undertaken too for the sake of its productivity, not only for the sake of the profit. Again, though, the economic order in which we live has now succeeded in identifying these two, so that men believe they cannot have one without the other. Here we must always reflect and reflect deply, in order to isolate for ourselves what the ethical goals really are. Profit is certainly not an ethical goal, however else one can conceive it.

The idea that a man might find his work a vocation, almost a calling, to which he may respond in a moral spirit is not, admittedly, a very common one. But still, the task here is not too different from what it is otherwise. One must find that work for which one is fitted and then seek to do that work in a dutiful way. The ethical accomplishments of staying faithful, honest, and zealous through all the temptations to be otherwise, can also be measured by reference to one's vocation. No man does more than this, ethically speaking, even if he is a master builder and worker, and no man, again, ethically speaking, ought ever to be content with less.

One cannot deny the need for changes in social organization. But both the conservatives who fear the change and the radicals who welcome it probably mistakenly conceive its importance. For neither the old nor the new organization can compel men to greater ethical responsibility and a loftier conception of human life. The moral values of work can be realized by each man for himself without any change in social institutions, for a moral man finds his responsibilities in the given situation. Morality cannot be postponed, and it cannot wait for a more perfect society to be realized. Morality is not, therefore, dependent upon organization but is dependent upon the subjectivity of the personality. Each man has to begin with himself. Irrespective of circumstances, then, we can echo Kierkegaard by saying that there is a pathos available for the wise and the unwise, the scholar and the plain man, the rich man and the poor man. This pathos and inwardness, present in our work and giving it substance, is the fact which to know is to know the essential democracy of human life.

MORALITY AND RELIGION

FROM WHAT HAS been said in the first three essays of this book, it might be concluded that the agnostic character of discursive learning on matters of morals is no serious obstacle after all. Morality is not a beggar gaining permission to live by gathering the crumbs falling from the feasts of learning. Morality has its resources deep within human personality. As has been noted, morality supposes an inner enthusiasm which may begin to flower with social pressure and other external demands but which ends by evaluating everything else in terms of choice. Unfortunately, religion sometimes functions as one of these external demands. The consequence is that it is assumed that spontaneity and choice-making are dampened by the application of religion, that morality and the sensitivity therein noted are incompatible with religious allegiance

However this is a gross error. For the moral consciousness is not contrary to religious consciousness; instead one can say that moral consciousness is incorporated wholly and entirely into religious consciousness. For religion too is, in part, an adventure of the inward man. Even though religious teachings are part of an historical heritage and even though churches and ways of attending to religious things are externally enjoined, still it is altogether proper on religious grounds and authority to point out that the aim of all these things is a new man, forgiveness of guilt, and the redintegration and renewal of the human creature. Just as the first disclosure of morality for many persons is the social pressure which activates behavior, so the first disclosure of religion is often the institution and its many sided activities. However, the consequent tends in an analogous direction, namely, of reshaping and reconstituting the inner life and grounding the religious behavior in faith, in hope, and in love, all of which are traits of the inner man.

The Religious Consciousness

First something must be noted of religious consciousness. One might hope that each reader will recognize that there is such a thing as religious consciousness. For surely it is not enough to characterize religion by describing religious institutions or religious laws or theology or even the observable qualities of devotion. There is also a kind of subject life, a kind of religious subjectivity, which is irreducible. Religious consciousness is not moral consciousness directed by an institution; neither is it simply moral consciousness directed to a divine object. Immanuel Kant argued a view something like that noted. He believed that a moral man's consciousness was describable by an obligation which was categorical rather than conditional. A moral man, in his view, would act out of considerations of duty alone and not in virtue of a calculation of the anticipated consequences. Religion was distinguished in the life history of a person by an addition to the awareness of obligation, but the addition was the conviction that the moral law was an expression of a divine will. Thus the thought of God is added via an attempt to ground the moral law in something besides oneself.

Perhaps this makes sense, though I suspect that people also believe in God because they have been told about him or have read about him in holy literature. Nonetheless, Kant is right in directing our gaze towards religious consciousness. For if religion is to be described at all, no one can afford to neglect the oddness of religious consciousness. This is not to say that such an account as follows is complete or even in principle could be a complete account of things religious. Such was the mistake of some theologians and theoreticians, like Schleiermacher and Feuerbach, who neglected the objective teachings of religion in their enthusiasm for the adventures within human subjectivity. The reflective man has a task before him if he chooses to describe morality and religion. The argument here is that the subject matter which is at hand and proximate to every man is the material provided by the inner life; and though it does not exhaust religion, it will serve us well to examine it in some detail.

No one with a sensitivity to the historical practices of Jews and Christians can deny that the rules and laws of a special community are intimate definers of a devoted Jew's personal life; and, likewise, the historical existence of Jesus surely focuses the energies and powers of Christians. Supposing these things, however, we shall ask whether the consciousness of Jews and Christians, and others too for that matter, is not itself transformed so that it becomes describably different.

Except in very special cases, a religious man is certainly under obligation. Religion provides no exemption from the common tasks and ordinary responsibilities. But there are a couple of factors added to ethical consciousness which get singular stress in the

religious life. One of them we can name simply as a sense of gratitude. The other has to do with a deepened sense of personal imperfection. The gratitude of which we here speak could also be called
a kind of receptivity wherein one views everything in life as a gift
as well as a task. Increasingly a religious man tends to apprehend
the relations between himself and his troubles, his neighbors, his
environment, not simply as the occasion for new tasks but also as
the occasion for thankfulness. Surely the Apostle Paul's words
about being thankful in all things are not meant to suggest that if
one is religious, 'things' will become better, but rather that in being religious (in this instance, Christian) the sense of gratitude
must grow no matter what the character of the things.

For this very reason, too, the sense of responsibility grows.
Every gift, for so the things of the world are then conceived, gives
rise to a task, and every task takes its departure in a gift. The doctrine of creation asserts these things on a cosmic scale. The
theme of that teaching is that everything that is, is a gift from God;
and furthermore that every gift is good. It is no mistake to say
then that the doctrine of creation is an expression of a deeply
religious consciousness in which a synthesis of cosmic gratitude
and personal responsibility is presupposed.

Most of us are taught the creation story long before we have
even begun to reflect upon ourselves and our place in the world.
It is no wonder then that such a story seems a little fanciful. Furthermore, many of us have been set to wondering whether the
story is true in virtue of evidence, whether Moses or someone
really saw those marvellous actions or not. Or did God inspire men
to write them down as they supposedly occurred? It is not mine

to rule on such questions. However, it is well to have one's attention drawn to what is otherwise so easily overlooked, namely, that the account is an expression of religious consciousness and not simply the cause thereof. Also, before the account can be put to any use in one's own life, before it can be believed, a spirit of thankfulness must be joined. The transformations of a person which lead to thankfulness as an attitude are many and subtle, but certainly thankfulness is essential to the religious life. Gratitude is a *sine qua non* of a religious man's subject life

This is accompanied by a deepened sense of personal imperfection. Often enough moral failures cause us to reflect upon our lack of opportunity, our miscalculations, our lack of insight and our plain mistakes in judgment. But a religious spirit views the failure and the task somewhat differently. The awareness of the need of changing the individual himself to fit him for the moral task grows even deeper. And the awareness of wrong-doing is transformed into a sense of guilt which is a concrete form for the sense of personal imperfection. The guilt is not in consequence simply of the disparity between "the ought" and "what is," for such guilt is properly speaking moral in character. Moral faults have their remedy in a correct action and the proper form of obedience. Religious guilt supposes that the wrongness is not only in the deed but in the doer, not in the mistaken action but in the man himself.

Hence there is, as Hegel and others have noted, a kind of negative aspect of self-consciousness in the religious man. The religious man is put in a position which appears dubious to the outsider, of feeling responsible for an imperfection which is greater than his wrong-doing. Furthermore, his guilt is not proportionate to the extent of his failures. This is why guilt in the religious man is so closely linked to suffering. For suffering here is the evidence that the self is being transformed in accordance with a pattern different from the obligations proffered by the social context. Perhaps there is no suffering quite so pervasive as this. The kind of perfection demanded is not that gained by obedience to command but rather a kind which is not summarized in precept nor abridged in social expectations

It is because the consciousness of a man can become like this that the language of religion is finally so different from the language of morality. While philosophers have often asked questions about the supposed objectivities, the laws, the commands, the rules, the social pressures, and the rest, which might conform a moral consciousness, they have not always found it easy to discuss moral consciousness itself. Immanuel Kant tried to do so and then failed lamentably to note that impulses, that inclinations, that social expectations among other things, do actually conspire to produce a moral consciousness. Kant was so intent upon discussing the consciousness of moral obligation that he looked for reasons for saying that nothing else, either objective and social or psychological and subjective, really mattered. The morality of which Kant speaks becomes so abstract that it no longer seems to inhere in our common life and ordinary humanity. Other philosophers, like John Stuart Mill and the utilitarians, become so intent upon correcting Kant's excesses that they tend to omit the peculiarities of moral consciousness altogether.

Recently the philosophers have turned to language itself as

the locus of philosophic problems. Undoubtedly many issues of reflection arise because we are not clear in speech, and our talking frequently makes matters worse rather than better. But, it is lamentable again if the preoccupation with language should blind us to the way men conceive and believe themselves to be and also to the way that they themselves actually are. Morality and religion have to do with motives, purposes, wishes; judgments about ourselves; hopes, and a variety of other traits. The numerous calls to belief, to allegiance, to obedience, to sympathy, to pathos, are not without their effect. We become moral persons in virtue of a history. Morality is learned, painfully and slowly, sometimes it appears almost inadvertently, but it is still learned. Religion is learned too. The Christian Scriptures make a point of this by differentiating between the first birth wherein we are born into the natural environment and a second birth wherein we are born into grace and a new set of motives. Whatever the merit of the circumlocutions, the point is an acknowledgment of the fact that the religious consciousness is not identical with naivete and innocence.

But this returns us again to the thought that religious consciousness is different than moral consciousness, which difference can be marked in our speech about guilt We shall note briefly a few problems about guilt before returning to our main theme.

Religious Guilt

On the one side it is clear that ethical men do speak about guilt; but guilt belongs properly to moral evil and is not like an error or a shortcoming. In legal contexts guilt belongs to a man when he has contravened the law of the people and when he deserves the penalty. However, an ethical man would not admit that legal guilt and ethical guilt are really the same. Surely it is possible to have one without the other. But this still demands that we conceive of guilt in a distinctive ethical sense.

Some theorists have been so impressed with the many psychological accompaniments of guilt that they have neglected the phenomenon itself. Because we blame people, some are inclined to argue that guilt is defined in the degree to which we can blame. Because we can condemn the conduct of others, it is sometimes said that guilt derives its significance from the condemnation. Consequently guilt is made out to be really psychological in genesis and is considered actually an effect, produced by a variety of attitudes such as blame, condemnation, remorse, anger, and indignation. Depending upon how one views guilt and its effect in turn upon people, it is conjectured that it can be produced and/or absented by psychological manipulation.

Such a view again denies perhaps the distinctively ethical character of guilt and the fact that there is an ethical conception of it, token of the ethical consciousness, not to be wholly delineated in psychological or legal language. It is correct to say that moral blaming and righteous indignation derive their significance from the conditions of moral evil, and the conditions of moral evil are the conditions of moral guilt. And men the world over give us a clue to the nature of moral sensitivity when they draw distinctions between their failures to master mathematics, or their inabilities to appreciate Scriabin, or their mistaken judgments about the price of wheat, and their moral wrong-doing. It is the latter which deserves and draws the guilt of men. The language of the world is replete on this point, and philosophers and ordinary men can discover little esoteric learning that suggests the right to depart therefrom. Obviously people do feel guilty, and a variety of distressing emotions are often the accompaniments. It seems implausible on the basis of the testimony of men about themselves to assume that the feeling of guilt is simply a vague premonition of consequences, or an inchoate fear of punishment. Despite the numerous endeavors to re-write the ethical talk that men perpetrate about themselves, sometimes to reduce it to psychological talk, sometimes to sociological, sometimes to theological, it seems to me we have every reason to take it very seriously simply as it stands.

Furthermore, we have access to moral things ourselves. Here we are not indebted to experts, however useful they might be in strictly intellectual matters. Every man is his own moral agent, and the moral cosmos is his own to explore. Perhaps it is needless to suggest then that every man, rich or poor, learned or ignorant, has a right to protest and to assert on some of these matters.

From these considerations, however, stems a confusion nevertheless. For the religious conception of guilt still proves to be somewhat different from the ethical conception. There are moralists who wish to deny this. Their attack is in principle similar to the attacks upon moral consciousness noted above, namely to reduce the religious definition and language to moral terms and to explain the religious consciousness in purely non-religious fashion.

A religious consciousness is pervaded, as earlier noted, by a sense of guilt. But in contrast to the ethical accounting, guilt here is not exclusively a function of moral evil. It may well begin there but it does not end there. The religious sense of guilt is not quantitative at all. This is why there is little heed to big sin and little sin, to specifying any commensurateness between degrees of objective evil and the psychological and inward sense of guilt. One might suppose that something like this in the instance of anxiety caused Freud to say that it was floating. Actually, however, guilt does not "float;" for the sense of guilt is pervasive and induces that kind of suffering and contrition within which a man understands himself to be guilty and imperfect. Evil in the moral understanding is always a variable and hence needs the quantitative description that the moralist demands; moral guilt, too, is a variable depending upon the degree of moral worth which one has denied or the moral evil which one has encompassed.

But such a calculus seems like a vain thing in so far as religious guilt is concerned. Gradually a religious consciousness learns to construe the guilt as total, including within its grasp both good and evil; both obedient and disobedient deeds. Thus the propensity, almost appearing natural, to compare successive moments and deeds in one's life history for purposes of determining moral worth is herewith defied. While it is certainly true that overt action is not a complete index to moral worth of persons, the religious man goes further and asserts that overt action, even if commendable, has no relation whatsoever to the degree of guilt. Such a guilt seems again not reducible to either moral dimensions or to the language of natural phenomena. Talk about guilt and sin being a taint upon one's nature, or being a state of ill-health, is not a very helpful analogy, especially when the religious consciousness is clear that there are no analogies.

Such a consciousness of guilt is an emergent in the life history of a subject. Whatever its antecedents, whatever its predisposing and precipitating causes, both as a "sense" of guilt and in its linguistic expressions, it remains a a factor not to be explained away. All the calculations of less and more, of the just and unjust action, become irrelevant either to establish or disestablish the guilt. For the effect of guilt here is to propose not the moral remedy alone, the moral deed in place of the immoral deed, but a new and even more taxing responsibility. The imperfection for which guilt is an expression cries out for a radical change within the individual himself.

Typically a religious consciousness also dares the belief in God. It is not appropriate here to remark upon all of the difficulties which are alleged by men of learning on this very ambiguous question. However, it is perhaps more appropriate to begin with the religious consciousness and all that helps form it than it is to begin with the fantastically odd question, Does God exist? Certainly the men who believe in God must have a clear and penetrating perspicacity with respect to themselves. And the latter, the self perspicacity, is prerequisite for the former, the belief in God. This negative aspect of self-consciousness, the sense of guilt, earned by moral endeavor though not totally defined thereby, is finally only appropriate if one is guilty in the presence of God. And then the new pattern begins to take shape. As the religious literature has already said and continues to say, so the guilt and the consequent suffering become evidence that the self is being transformed in accordance with a pattern higher than justice and obligation can define, and this pattern is God.

However, the issue is still the relation between morality and religion. It has been argued that one way to see the relation is to see it in the inward man. Also, it has been asserted that religious consciousness distinguishes the sense of imperfection in such a manner that it can no longer be described within ethical categories.

Religious Justification

There is still another odd kind of connection between morality and religion. Perhaps it needs a little more explanation. Almost all men have discovered that anything spoken or written can be challenged. When we are told something, we are usually supposed to believe it. Believing something that someone has said has its risks and uncertainties, and it does not demand much intelligence to ask for substantiation, for evidence, and for proof. Deception is rife among us, and there are few indeed who have not been fooled just enough to learn to ask for more than the same thing said over again. Out of this kind of experiencing and talking grows the quest for the justified beliefs, those which are warranted and worthy of acceptance.

Initially this is not very complicated. Certainly it is very instructive to observe ourselves here and to note that we do not behave as the books on logic and correct thinking seem to say. Most of us are not actually looking for evidence when we doubt somebody's word nor are we busy pursuing proofs. These are the logicians' ways of talking about what we actually do. But each person must test himself here and forego the temptation of casting all of his ways of assuring himself into a common shape and style. Nonetheless, all of us can be and are dubious about things said to us, and we want and seek a kind of justification for what is said, though there seems to be a wide variety of ways of regaining assurance about what is said.

We can suppose that the intellectual life of a man does not really begin until a little doubt insinuates its way into everything we read and hear. If everything is so because it is said, the intelligence stays rather dormant and is seldom aroused save by the extravagant, the ludicrous, or the bizarre. But when we 'think,' we have to search out something and, not least, the very justification for our beliefs and our talk. It is no mistake to take pedagogy very seriously; for a skillful teacher's responsibility is not simply to fill the empty "noggins" in front of her, but also to rouse the intelligence from torpor and to help search out the valid and justified in place of the unwarranted and invalid. To have the bearing of the intelligent man is certainly to seek out whatever it is that justifies believing.

This consideration is, though, only an avenue to considering an ethico-religious concern for which we sometimes use the same word. For religion and morality also find the word justification very useful. In the context of morality, we talk about justifiable behavior, justifiable action, and even whether a policy was really justified. Sometimes we may be only speaking indirectly and about beliefs which need justification; but more likely, and in ordinary ways of talking, we refer to and judge men and deeds as to their warrantability, their worth and validity. Perhaps it is moot again to remark that such judgmental language undoubtedly should be used about oneself rather than others, though the latter reference appears almost inescapable in social life where moral concerns are omnipresent.

Earlier it was remarked that there was a deep seated need in men for a justifiable way of life. Surely the sense of obligation drives a man in the direction of a righteous and defensible way of life. Moral consciousness is distinguished by this relentless and ceaseless pursuit for a completely valid and perfected selfhood. Albeit this is quite different from a valid thought, important though a thought might also be. Furthermore, there seem to be no intrinsic and inevitable relations between thinking validly and correctly and being a morally valid person. Justification is not transferable from one to other. The same kind of gap seems to loom up between justification in intellectual matters and moral affairs as looms up between the awareness of making a mistake in arithmetical calculation and the awareness of guilt relative to a moral wrong.

So, we might conclude again that moral consciousness is distinguished by evaluating human life in terms of choice, that it does indeed view all conduct in terms of obligation and duty; that is, that it penetrates all particulars with a spirit of universality. But something additional can now be said, namely that moral consciousness views existing as a task in which the justification and vindication, the very defensible righteousness, of a man is won or lost. All of this moral severity is brought into religious consciousness too, but again a differentiation occurs. For a religious man never loses the need for righteousness nor is he exempted from the requirement of blamelessness. But gradually again another theme is added, and this is to the effect that a justification and a valid existence cannot really be achieved. The consciousness of guilt teaches a person that the justified life is an evanescent goal, that the imperfection is more deeply rooted than the moral tasks presuppose, that justification, if it comes at all, must come as a gift and not as an achievement.

So here it might be seen again that guilt in a religious consciousness tokens the invalidity of the person, not simply the failure of a deed or an act. Guilt is an expression for that kind of consciousness which understands the self to be imperfect and in need of justification. It is well to mark the fact that any person can reflect about himself and note these things. One of the character-istics of a sincere man is the exercise of the capacity to think about himself and discover some of these things, not least his guilt. Many people, including many an otherwise distinguished genius of reflection, take existence for granted, and all of its substantial factors.

Most people bestow their thought on relativities. To think about oneself in the manner noted above is to think about the essentials. Thus it is that there is an almost universal chorus of approval upon the reality and validity of norms for the relativities like being a professor, a scientist, a doctor, a policeman, or even a warden at Sing Sing. But the recognition of a norm for man as man, most men like to deny. Everywhere there is the polite decrier who denies that there is anything to learn here or who says that what norms there are, are only dogmatic assertions. This is the point of declaring that all valuations are in the last analysis only arbitrary decisions and conventional choices. Such things are also said about the religious man's thesis of personal guilt. Some would assert simply that the sense of guilt indicates only the factual existence of a feeling of guilt, and hence a claim to validity is relevant. Perhaps the fundamental warrant that a man has for taking the consciousness of guilt seriously as a claim arises only when valuation and the need for the achievement of validity and justification in the happiness they seek become a concrete life-problem, and not a problem for authors in general or an issue in epistemology.

God and Man

Out of all this one can understand again how it is that the God-idea stands related to morality. Surely it is true that the gift without the giver is bare, and men become supernaturalists accordingly. The God-idea of a morally achieved religiousness cannot help be personal, almost as a matter of course. No other God-idea could possible do justice to a man's needs and to the nature of morality itself. The God-idea is a personality-category, for as moral men have long since discovered, personality is the only abiding value. This is why religion so seldom finds or seeks a basis for the God-idea in the abstractions of physics or the reflections about a first-cause or a Prime Mover. It seeks instead the basis for the idea of God in the depths of the human heart.

Men can ill afford therefore to give up the task of thinking about themselves, their goals, their validity, their future and its tasks. Here is where the greatness, such as we ever have it, really lies. We must idealize our personal relationships. The highest sort of religion even makes faith a concrete personal attitude, and this kind of faith has as its object a concrete personal attitude, a God who is love and a person.

If we think about these things it becomes clear again that religion stripped of the ethical components becomes poetry or metaphysics. And when religion is stripped of the sense of gratitude or receptivity and its cognate category, imperfection, it becomes a crude kind of externalism and even politics. The religious man owns to the fact that he needs to reconstitute the integrity of his entire personality. Without this need, it is almost as if he has failed to recognize what he is. It is, therefore, only thoughtlessness which sees guiltlessness as superior to guilt, for guilt is the sign of one's ethical majority. When one remembers that the experience of justification in religion, imputed though it be, is achieved, it must be remembered that a new standard and measure for human reconciliation is also proposed. The consciousness of divine forgiveness is lost to us when we refuse to forgive our enemies or those who have done us an injury. Here too we see how the deepened sense of receptivity conditions a deepened activity and task, a more penetrating consciousness of the moral task and ideal.

To observe that all of these things are not accidents of fortune nor caprices of the aristocrat is to note that these things are available to every man. All that is required is the courage to face the fact that morality and even religion do not live by the cognitive certainties. Here there is struggle and strife, objective uncertainty and doubt, discipline and suffering. But this is how expensive the best things of life, the ethico-religious qualities, really are. It is not finally the extent of talent, of genius and fortune, which deter-

mine the moral life and its victories. Here the victory goes to the
strugglers who achieve the inevitable sense of heterogeneity within themselves, and with the spirit dominant in the world; but, who,
nonetheless, win the happiness of looking back upon sufferings
endured in a good cause.

www.ingramcontent.com/pod-product-compliance
Lightning Source LLC
Chambersburg PA
CBHW062025040426
42447CB00010B/2135